Start a Business with No Money

"If you get offered an opportunity and don't know how to do it, Just say yes and work out how to do it later" Richard Branson

The Inception

A seed was sown 6 months ago during a drive to London for business.

I don't know about you but I tend to find that during driving I do one of two things. Immerse myself in an audible book to try and maximise my personal development
The second is to think about ideas and concepts and look at ways in which to turn thoughts into a reality and ultimately a vision of the future

This book is one of those thoughts and through those thoughts I created massive action which in turn has manifested itself as what you read here today

I hope you enjoy reading through the concept and appreciate the small part you are playing in my ultimate vision!
And if not there is a sneeky bribe somewhere in the book so you will have to read the whole thing to find it!

Well you can't get something for nothing there is always a transaction in everything you do in life!

Why write a book?

People don't throw books away they keep them so keep your little piece of history safe and you will be able to say you were there at the beginning!

Disclaimer

This book is in no way a definitive guide to building your business and by the end you will fully understand why it has been written.
After listening to a large quantity of personal development books I wondered how many ideas became books before they became reality.

I wondered if any of the people who write about becoming successful in business have only become successful in business by writing about it first. The proverbial Chicken v Egg Theory

Buy reading this far you have hopefully become part of what I can only describe as potential history as all of the greatest business have started from nothing and people have been innovative and tenacious in their own pursuits of success.

I am hoping to break a paradigm or attract the investment of philanthropist keen to find out what I am truly capable of so feel free to get in touch via one of the contact details I have provided throughout this book

What it does is outline some of the fundamentals to starting your business and provide you with some interesting insight into how I have started mine

This is in fact the second Business I have started from nothing with no capital and in two different industries.

The first started as a self-employed sales role which now spans two cities here in the UK.
This role taught me a fantastic amount about the mentality required to start a business and run it successfully.

From all the different books I have read and listened to Mentality and making specific demands/goals with a vison of what is going to manifest is the key then surround yourself with the people capable of making it happen.

This entire book is based on my own personal opinion and does not reflect that of any of the people quoted in this book. It will cover some of the Personal thought processes I have encountered during the set up phase.
I would like to thank some of the people who have inspired me to start this business.

Some through negativity and triggering my stubborn streak, some through inspiring me through their personal stories and books, some through personal encouragement.

What do you want?

If you are going into business for the money then you will be shocked over the first few years as without passion for what you are looking to create you will fall down at the first hurdle. You must have some clearly defined goals you are working towards at different milestones.

You must have a reason to do what you are doing that is far beyond personal gain financially
Think of profit as the fruit and your business as the seed to a mighty fruit tree.
There is a lot of input required before your tree is mature enough to bear fruit in abundance.
The more work you put in to caring for the business and feeding it what it needs to grow strong from the base the larger and more stable the business will become.

We have all seen the financial storm blow through the business world over the last 10 years and blow over some very large trees and I personally do not plan on being one of them the next time this happens.

The trick is to create multiple income streams unfortunately 95% of people rely on the one role they take up exchange there time for money and if that method fails they have nothing.
By taking the step into running your own businesses you are not only taking control and responsibility for your income but also protect yourself and your family against the future regardless on how the world turns financially.

Timing

This is the perfect time to start a business!

After a recessional clear out of businesses there is plenty of space for people to start their own venture. Some of the greatest businesses have been created by people looking to generate an income when they are short on work.

TEA UN-LIMITED

"A GREAT CUP OF TEA"

How to start a business with no capital and without lending money from Investors or the Bank.

Why would you want to be able to do this?

For me this was a desirable option as it gives me choices. The choices increase the larger the initial capital you can accumulate.

The first thing you need is a goal.
This goal needs to be a specific target of start up money you require to get up and running.

BUSINESS PLAN

My business plan is very simple

I am going to try and emulate the success of the big coffee chains for example Costa/Starbucks and simply sell tea instead

I decided to adapt a business plan for a coffee and expresso Bar as there are many online for me to work from as a base and then develop the areas where I am going to stand out.

Draft Version
(Not so confidential)
Version 1

Tea Un-Limited

Business Plan

2015

Executive Summary

Tea Un-Limited is a speciality tea shop concept based on a broad and creative selection of Tea based beverages. Tea Un-Limited provides a new tea experience by creating a recognised environment to enjoy speciality tea beverages and making tea drinking an end in itself. This concept is different from anything present in the UK tea shop/bar Market today.

Tea Un-Limited offers its customers not just Black tea and its other popular variants, but a host of exciting herbal, fruit tea and Iced Tea.
These drinks are created and served by trained "T'xpert" who will act more like a skilled cocktail barman than your average "tea lady"
As a Compliment to the tea offerings Tea Un-Limited will also serve a basic selection of coffee, juices, cakes and biscuits

Tea Un-Limited Concept although unique in its market has been very successful in other formats namely Coffee in the form of Costa and Starbucks who have expanded expansively in the beverage industry

There are billions of cups of tea consumed here in the UK but no recognised high street brand where you can guarantee quality throughout the UK
This is something Tea Un-Limited plan to exploit with the scope to take the internationally within 5 years through franchising following the proven Mc Donald's model

The following 5 points are what will differentiate Tea Un-Limited from the competition

First the definition of competition
1. Coffee Bars such as Café Nero, Costa, Starbucks
2. Traditional Tea rooms

Tea is still the most widely drank hot beverage in the UK with some indication that people often buy a coffee based on the fact the tea they sell is awful

Tea rooms tend to be very quirky and bespoke to the owner and have regular clientele which tends to be restricted to local knowledge or clever locations

Unique Selling Points

1. All the comfort of a Coffee Bar But with the predominant beverage being Tea

2. The first recognisable high street Tea brand
3. Unique Merchandising and Marketing
4. Convenient locations with prominent positioning
5. Good Cup Of Tea

The initial company structure will be set up to provide a strong range of skills
Developing a range of staff from the ground up coaching them in the ethics and the Tea Un-Limited Way

Although this is the initial strategy we will be looking to expand aggressively using strong links with the Princes Trust to offer s strong business foundation for young entrepreneurs to be able to grow their own franchise chain coupled with coaching and support through continuous development

Charity Built In

Due to my forces background I will form a firm partnership with Forces Focused charities particularly those dedicated to post traumatic stress as I personally have struggled with PTSD as a lot of friends it seems to be claiming as many lives as the wars themselves. I wish to offer an ever increasing funding stream to help the charity continue to deliver the amazing work for our armed services
(On Stateside expansion this will switch allegiances to American Forces focussed charities for the American side of the business)
The secondary side to this is to offer opportunities to ex-service men and women

I Will also be looking to work closely with the likes of the Princes Trust to help nurture the young entrepreneurs of the future

With the increasing revenue of this book and the income generated by the business we will look to expand to capitalise on the economies of scale both operationally and through dynamic Marketing

The sequel to this book will be generated and sold to help generate the initial expansion costs. The goal is to continue to be cash rich making us a very dynamic start up with no financial liability while establishing ourselves as the premier hot beverage business in the UK before taking over the world.

Marketing and Merchandising

This section I am going to keep under my hat for the time being but be rest assured as clever as writing a book about the start up to generate revenue to actually start this business.

My marketing and merchandising strategies will hold equal levels of resourceful outside the box thinking and I wouldn't want to give the competition a head start in that side of things

Customer Service

Tea Un-Limited are going to recruit internally to begin with to eliminate un necessary costs associated with recruitment but may look to outsource as an account to a national provider when the business becomes more established

The goal is to build a training structure and environment where people look forward to working not unlike the Apple and Google office environments

Training will be intensive and thorough with the goal of becoming industry recognised as un-beatable through providing a customer focused experience

The uniform will clean shirts bearing the company Logo including Email

Store design will be very similar to the regular coffee shop designs we see everywhere today helping keep a familiar feel for new customers

We will be looking to accommodate a high footfall but also re inforce a calm relaxed atmosphere with comfortable functional seating areas for the less busy

Initial shop design and manufacture will be done on a budget to ensure value for money.

Site Selection and Location

All sites will be strategically placed in visible areas with high footfalls
The mid-term goal will be to target the motorway service station, airport and railway stations to get maximum impact on the country as the go to retail outlet for a good cup of tea.

Initially we will search and select areas where there appears to be a low penetration of incumbent coffee retailers but in time boldly take them on in a full frontal high street assault. We will look to dominate the UK Hot beverage market within 5 years.

Supplies

Tea

Other offerings

Operations and Management

Initially each store will require a manager and 2 full time members of staff although through monitoring footfall and sales extra staff may be rotated in to maximise efficiency during these times.

The Staff will operate like a well-oiled machine being an expert in their specific function.

Taking the order, producing the order, delivering the product.

Initially Tea Un-Limited will open between 07:00 and 19:00 but this will be adjusted to the location

All members of staff must be in uniform with a name badge.

Tea Un-Limited
"A Great Cup of Tea"

Thank You. You won't know why I have thanked you yet but you will when you get to the end of my book.

Chapter 0 lets get started

Identifying a problem you are passionate about solving.

Question: Where can I get a great cup of tea?

On the back of this question a number of you may instantly think of a lovely little tea room near where you live or work and I am not in any way talking about them.

The Seed Of An Empire

November 3 2014 I was travelling to London from Nottingham for a business meeting and decided on route I fancied nice cup of tea to break up the journey.

I currently run a Direct Marketing Business canvassing customers with different products and services. Yes the kind of person who will come and knock on your door and introduce you to different things. Some you will like and want to buy. Some you will like and want to think about it. Some you are not interested. The latter two both mean NO.

I work on the Law of Averages which if you do something enough times you will find the results. I guess its an effective way of sieving the country for different clients in a very cost effective way.

So whether you agree with it or not it is a very effective way of getting your product out into the market place. (The interesting thing is if you are reading this book there is a very good chance you will have been sold it by me in person on a Sunday afternoon by the end you will understand why)

Back to the story Now I stopped off at the services and found that they only have one of the big branded Coffee Houses which seem to have appeared everywhere. I may go off on a little rant now as this is something I am very passionate about.

I am British. I am proud to be British. I support the Queen. I spent 9 ½ years in Her Majesties Armed Forces serving both here in the UK and abroad.

I DRINK TEA!

One of the most annoying things is having to buy a cup of tea from one of the coffee shops. Why? Because they are generally awful in my personal opinion.

Perhaps this is about to secure me a death threat or two from the caffeine fuelled self-proclaimed coffee snobs but I really dislike coffee. At best I would require 4 sugars and a few shots of Irish Cream to make it mildly bearable.

Obviously Alcoholic coffee with enough sugar to wire me to the moon was not advisable due to the fact I had an hour left to drive which left me no choice but to brave the substance referred to as tea from one of these coffee outlets.

Three sips confirmed that I had again wasted my money and the nearest refuse receptacle was utilised to its fullest.

Concept

Idea "why is there nowhere nationally recognisable for me to get a great cup of tea in a country of stereotyped tea drinkers"

So a few weeks passed and I was again on my travels and heading with my entire business to a large conference with lots of other positive like-minded sales people.

One of the speakers I have to say was an inspiration and I had a "lightbulb" moment.

Sahar Hashemi one of the Brother and Sister team who Built Coffee Republic. Sahar Talked about a trip to New York where she visited a Starbucks coffee shop and how she was inspired by all the confectionary delights and amazing coffee and how there was nothing like that here in the UK so set about bringing this to our shores.

I see her as the original Grey Squirrel invading the UK with coffee but she hit home a very good point of which I find myself 20 years after the first coffee republic opening having the same questions about tea! Where on the high-street is there a recognisable brand of tea so this is my mission to create the foundations of a franchisee Tea Empire

THE LIGHT BULB MOMENT

What will we sell? A Great Cup Of Tea!

Now this may seem a simple enough challenge as in fact it really is a very basic concept and from the years I have worked in Direct sales the simple ideas are more often than not the best ones.

The Concept of Tea Un-limited was born!

Market Research

My entrepreneurial problem is that I have a very excitable imagination and I got that burning feeling in my gut that this idea is both fantastic and ingenious.

My mind had already opened up 15-20 stores across 4 cities and already looked at how the expansion was going to get stuck into the US growing market for tea the more I thought about it the bigger the idea got and the more feasible it sounded this time next year we are going to be as big as Starbucks I was telling myself and floating on the stock market for £100 billion.

1. We are a nation of tea drinkers
   Did you know we drink 165 million cups of tea each day as a nation? That is 60.2 Billion per year
   Are we a nation of coffee drinkers?
   No only 70 million cups of coffee are drunk on a daily basis. (Some of which because a good cup of tea is not yet available)
2. For every coffee shop there is in the UK I could have a Tea shop
3. Tea Un-Limited Merchandise
4. Tea Un-Limited Tea + Infusions in superstores
5. I can franchise it to Young entrepreneurs within the princes trust and help put more jobs into the country
6. I could donate a proportion of Profits to charity
7. Expand into the US
   Did you know in 2014 Americans consumed over 80 billion cups of tea imagine a UK tea brand that they recognise from visits to the uk became readily available for them back home
8. Iced tea for the summer
9. Tea is a good healthy option of drink containing less caffeine than a cup of coffee and a number of antioxidants
10. Tea Un-limited Hotel/Airline/Business Partnerships
    Thankfully I have friends who like to keep my feet on the ground so this is chapter 0 the start

FACTs

I am writing this book before the first store has even opened

Before the first website has been registered and even before I have registered as a Limited company

Why? Well its simple all start ups require capital so this is what is going to generate the money to get us off the ground.

This could be seen as a crazy idea letting the cat out of the bag before we even have a bag let alone the cat to put in it but hey if someone wants to steal the concept and get rocking that's all fine with me competition is key and I look forward to hearing the conversations between the "tea snobs" arguing which chain does the best tea.

Starting Capital

Target Basic (£100,000) Ideal (£250,000)

So there are a number of things we need to get started.

A location £50,000 annually

Furnishing a shop to be similar to the coffee chains £20,000 – £50,000

Water and Electric £500 per month

Staff £35,000

Business rates (variable)

Corporation Tax on profits 20% (18%)

Charity

You may think I am crazy on a different level by putting charity in my start-up costs so please indulge me on an altruistic view

I firmly believe what is going to stand us out from the crowd on a number of levels is that I am factoring in 10% of profits will be donated to Forces focused Charity. Forces Chariti are very close to my heart having served in Afghanistan

With the retraction from conflict the Army is not in the news nearly as much as it once was for obvious reasons. Unfortunately the aftermath of the conflicts does not go away so easily so I would like this future multi-national to have a link to something I truly believe is important to the extent that when expansion to the US happens the charity will switch to an American Forces Focused Charity as I spent some time with them working out of Camp Tombstone in 2007

If the business is built with this element in place it will sustain itself

I would like to include that this will be a business model which accommodates ex forces and encourage them to drive and take on business ventures with our support through franchising in the coming years

Furthermore through this whole process I have decided that working alongside the princes trust we will be able to help secure gainful employment and business opportunities for young people in this country today

You may have realised I have mentioned them twice now but I feel them to be very important points to me.

Well now for the interesting part on securing funding

Unfortunately I am too old to be able to work with the Princes Trust on a personal level which I was a little disappointed

I have tried to pitch to Rich this year but have to admit my pitch was a little rubbish and very last min. com

Hopefully he will buy a copy of this book

I have applied for the apprentice and even tried to source Lord Sugar personally.

Interestingly my first interview after leaving the army was a long day down at a crown plaza in London auditioning for a place on the apprentice.

 I did meet the blonde lass who won it that year on the day but I can't remember her name for the life of me.

Dragons Den was another instant application I then tried to track down some of the dragons

One of the office did reply to explain she was quite busy and I suddenly realised I am not the only person looking for start-up capital.

I then started looking at the Banks and start-up funds it was then that I found out I had an awful credit rating. Some silly decisions from the past 2-3 years had come rearing back up to bite me from behind so I decided to knuckle down to work and save the capital myself

One of the joys of direct sales is that the money you earn is just cash you don't really have to worry about products or materials as these are generally provided by the client and in a commission only world you get back what you put in.

Whats so special about Tea here in the Great Britain

How tea is drunk today?

Britain enjoys an intimate love affair with tea – just look at the facts. On average we each drink 3½ cups of tea a day, or 130,000 tonnes in a year, 96 per cent of which are from tea bags. As a nation we drink 165 million cups per day or 62 billion cups per year; 70 per cent of the population (over the age of 10) drank tea yesterday; over 25 per cent of all the milk consumed in the UK goes in your cups of tea.

In the two minutes or so it has taken to type these two paragraphs, the tea-ometer on the Tea Council UK website has clocked up a staggering 191,000 cups of tea drunk in the UK; 70 million cups will have been made today by 11am.

Tea has become quintessentially British. It slowly but surely insinuated itself into our culture, language and society.

Even on the silver screen British people are always refered to as Tea Drinkers.

Tea is everywhere: afternoon tea, high tea, tea gowns, tea cakes, tea towels, tea gardens, tea dances, Lyons tea houses, tea-time, tea services, tea breaks, tea for two, storms in tea cups, builders' tea, more tea vicar? In the Military there are even phrases to describe what you are having

Standard NATO (as if issued from the storeman) Tea Two Sugars

Our loss of the American colonies (think the Boston Tea Party), votes for women, and victory in the two world wars – all owe something to a nice cup of tea.

Tea Controversy!

Question do you put in the milk first or not?

British Culture

Our culture is infused with tea and tea-time

Boy George famously quoted that he preferred a cup of tea to sex

Children's story books, The Tiger Who Came To Tea.

The Beatles wooed Lovely Rita Meter Maid with it;

The Kinks quote "It's a cure for hepatitis, it's a cure for chronic insomnia, it's a cure for tonsillitis and for water on the knee" in the group's song Have A Cuppa Tea.

One of the Rolling Stones' "nasty habits" was taking "tea at three" in their song Live With Me.

The wartime film Brief Encounter had many romantic cups of tea between its stars Trevor Howard and Celia Johnson.

The author George Orwell (an obsessive tea drinker) identified 11 rules for perfect tea-making, rules from which nobody should dare depart,

He Published these in the Evening Standard 12th January 1946 Orwell said that tea – one of the "mainstays of civilisation" in his opinion – is ruined by putting sugar in it and that anyone who does this could not be called "a true tea-lover".

First Ever tea break

How did it all start? Once upon a time, when the emperor Shen Nung was travelling to a far-fl ung province, he and his entourage stopped for a break, the world's very fi rst tea break as it turned out. Shen Nung , a scientist, knew how important it was to boil all drinking water; accordingly, the servants began to boil the water as they sat in a grove of camellia sinensis trees. The place was central China, the date was 2737BC, around the same time as the Egyptians started work on the pyramids of Giza.

The world's first herbal tea, and an exploding stomach

That day, however, was to be very special: a gentle breeze blew some leaves from the camellia sinensis into the emperor's cauldron of water; Shen Nung then took a sip of what was to be the world's first cup of tea. He liked it, it caught on, took the name "tea" and has become one of the most celebrated discoveries the world has known.

But it was not just the trajectory of the breeze-blown leaves that was fortuitous; Shen Nung happened to be a noted herbalist. A bit of a workaholic, he personally tested thousands of medicinal herbs, some of which were poisonous.

He went on to use his newly discovered tea as an antidote to 70 or so toxic herbs. But tea could not save him from the life-limiting consequences of his final experiment: one herb turned out to be particularly nasty: he ate it and his stomach exploded, according to legend. Shen Nung is today revered as the father of Chinese medicine and the discoverer of tea.

The Tea bag

Where did the tea bag come from? In 1908, New York tea merchant Thomas Sullivan hit on the idea of sending samples of tea out in small silk bags. Some recipients believed that these worked like his metal infusers and so immersed the bags into the pot, rather than emptying out the contents, as intended. Result: the tea bag.

The story of our intimate relationship with tea is in effect the social history of Britain. Tea: Like the noted 18th-century man of letters and compiler of the English language's first dictionary Samuel Johnson, we just can't get enough of it: "You cannot make tea so fast as I can gulp it down," he once said. So put the kettle on, put your feet up and have that nice cup of tea. As the Chinese proverb goes: "A day without tea is a day without joy."

The reality of this Book

It was then in dawned on me whilst listening to the secret that some of these guys had made a lot of money by selling the idea of being successful as there product so here we are today.

So are they successful before talking about success or did they become successful talking about success then selling the book?

How did the keep off the grass sign get there?

Are we alone in the universe?

Do penguins have knees?

I made the decision to start a series of books into my business and then film it at each stage the proceeds from this book today is in effect my start-up capital for the Tea Empire I am going to create.

The interesting thing will be should this be successful I will write a further instalment this time next year and let you in on some of the little extras we are keeping in the bag for our growth and you will be able to come and visit my first shop here in Manchester.

What came first the chicken or the egg? Or in this case the tea shop or the book!

I believe I will be the first Entrepreneur to have published a book on entrepreneurship before realising their goal which in itself is a freshly broken paradigm

All the graphics and illustration has also been done by me so you may notice a missing artistic link between my brain and my hand

Lastly Thank You again for helping my dreams and visions to have the chance of becoming a reality

By the time this book is published you will be able to visit our website

www.tea-unlimited.com

Seb@thehurricaneorganisation.co.uk

Tea Un-Limited

Sales Target 20,000 copies in 3 months please come and visit us either on line or in store we are coming to a highstreet near you!

My Goal From this Book

The Money I will be generating is **£250,000**
This is a large goal and I have a few reasons I have set it at this level

1. By setting a large goal if I fall short I will still have plenty of capital to get the ball rolling
2. Without lending money my business starts in the black ensuring cash flow over the first few years of business
3. The larger the quantity the larger the choices I have never run a business of this type so I want the ability to be able to act and do what my business needs free from financial constraint
4. With the projected growth the first wave of expansion will have money in place to put in the infrastructure
5. Ultimately You will be able to get a good cup of tea from a newly recognisable brand on the high street

Thank you

By purchasing this book you have in fact contributed to the capital I am using to start my business

The secret to building a business without capital or investment in this case is quite very simple I have created a book from the thought process of starting my tea shop empire and put it out there for all to read

At this stage I have no idea how much revenue I will generate from the written word and I have been described a completely crazy by many of my friends or mentors for even attempting this.

If you have enjoyed what you have read then please recommend my book to fiends and colleagues as the more books that are purchased the faster my start-up will get off the ground.

I hope you will follow my company keenly through social media or even in person by frequenting one of the shops to see what you have personally helped to create.

Anything you have read in this book I have read on the internet or sourced through amazing Audible books and books on Amazon.

This is by far the only book I have ever written and I hope you have enjoyed the read and are encouraged by my outside the box approach to securing the funds

The more copies we sell the fast and bigger my business will grow and you have been a part of it.

If you bring a copy of this book into a Tea Un-Limited Store we will gladly stamp it and provide you with a free cup of tea and a piece of shortbread for your support

I OWE YOU.

1 x Reg. Hot Beverage

1 x Shortbread

Served By

. . . .

Thanks to the following

Mum and Dad for always discouraging me from following my goals this has been one of the greatest fuels in my fire to prove you wrong and change the families lives forever I truly thank you from the bottom of my heart for showing me an amazing work ethic through my childhood I look forward to retiring you both and showing you what you have created through me!

All my Love.

Business Mentors within the direct sales world for being my business mentors and all the team, Wwho have played such a big part in my development so far. You guidance has been exceptional especially through times where I have doubted myself. Sue you strength of character has be amazing and I look forward to holding some Purple Heart events for Linz.and countless more inspirational business owners within the group who have helped direct the way I think (Desire Determines Destination) ;-)

Richard Branson for not letting me pitch you for investment forced me to really look outside the box for investment. I hope our paths cross in the future

Lord Sugar. For not letting me past the group stage of the apprentice 2007.

I would also Like to thank a girl who reminded me of one of the basic rules of starting a business

Stop talking about it and just go and do it

Thank you for anyone else who I haven't mentioned I apologise if I have forgotten you I wrote this list on a Sunday afternoon and the entire book was written between 7/5/2015 and 10/5/2015

I would also like to take this time to advertise

If you see yourself becoming part of my vision either here in the UK or our international expansion please do not hesitate to contact us

We are looking for **Staff, Budding Entrepreneurs, Investors, Business development Managers/ Team members, Recruiters, Franchisees, Account managers, Suppliers**

If you feel you might wish to join our **Tea Empire**

info@tea-unlimited.com (August 2015)

seb@thehurricaneorganisation.co.uk

Seb Hussey (Linked in)

The sequel to this book will come after 12-18 months of year one!

Tea Un-Limited "A great Cup of Tea" www.tea-unlimited.com

Final Thought

To start a business you need to be Resourceful, Tenacious, Resilient Passionate and very driven to make it work.

In the words of Nike "Just Do It"

We also have a Crowd Funding page

www.Crowdfunder.co.uk/tea-un-limited